# The Smart Entrepreneur's Guide to Social Networking

**Greg Pitstick**
**Bill Brown**

9378 Mason Montgomery Rd,
Suite 218
Mason, Ohio 45040

ISBN 1451500173
LCCN:2010903464

Printed in the United States of America.

# Acknowledgments

We would like to express our gratitude to those who have helped to make this book possible. First, we want to thank all our great coaching clients who have worked with us over the years to implement our marketing ideas, and ultimately validate their value of using social networking in actual business operations. We especially want to single out Bryan Casteel, the best real estate agent in Cincinnati, for working with us to implement what has become the core of our marketing approach. Thank you.

We want to thank those that helped to bring our book to life in its physical form. To Carmen Hudson, who helped us to organize our thoughts and materials into a book. To Brian Azhar, for his most excellent book cover design. And finally, to Julianne Geiger who cleaned up the mess we grammar-challenged authors created.

We also want to thank the late Bud Johnson of Yellow Springs, Ohio, who saw something special in the sickly kid others called Brace. Bud's willingness to share the gift of confidence and trust in Greg, and his many lessons about how to successfully run a small business changed to course of Greg's life—and by extension, the lives of countless others who became Greg's clients and partners in business.

And most importantly, we want to thank our loving wives and children who have tolerated our long hours and (sometimes) crazy ideas and have given us nothing but unfailing support in return.

# Preface

So, who am I and why should you listen to me? This is always a good question to ask when venturing into new ways of doing business.

First, understand that I am not a technical genius, nor am I an ivory-tower professor. I was not born to a millionaire, I don't have special technical skills, nor do I have superhuman interpersonal skills. In fact, I am a lot like you.

I grew up in the small town of Yellow Springs, Ohio, before anyone had a cell phone, used an ATM, or even heard of the Internet. Social networking was something that happened at the local bar, diner, or church festival.

In high school, I struggled to get much more than a C in many of my classes. I can tell you about my summer school experience, or my attempt to explain to my parents how on earth I could get a D in shop. I was on the road to a factory job in one of GM's plants in Dayton, Ohio.

My parents tried to remedy the situation with tutors, extra help, and even a psychiatrist to evaluate my potential (after drawing some pictures she said I was thinking too far ahead). I can still remember hearing my freshman algebra teacher, Mr. Hassmann, tell my parents that I could never learn algebra and should quit trying.

Alas, my parents did not give up. Instead, they took me to specialist after specialist, who always seemed find some problem that needed to be fixed (some real, some not so real).

To start with, I had a condition called Kyphosis (my back was curved forward—think: *old man hunched forward*), so I spent my junior and senior years in high school in a full back brace that began at my waist and continued up and around my neck. To exacerbate things, my teeth were quite crooked, so I had braces with hooks, wires, and rubber bands. I also have flat feet and I had special appliances for my shoes. Somewhere along the line, they discovered that I had a vision problem and needed bifocals. Of course, to top it off, I had weekly allergy shots and had to avoid certain foods. You get the picture. Needless to say, my nickname was *Brace*.

I couldn't play sports and had no music ability (and don't ask me to dance), so I got a job at the local drugstore. The store was straight out of the 1950s, and connected to the local diner. I worked every day after school (including Saturday mornings) and every summer throughout my high school career. A cranky old pharmacist named Bud Johnson was the owner.

Bud knew the secrets of running a successful business in good times and in bad, and he ran the most successful store in town. Bud's children were grown and he took a liking to me. Over the years, he shared his business knowledge and techniques with me and taught me some of the most important lessons of my life.

- First – You can only achieve what you believe. If you listen to the negative voices in your life, you will never achieve the greatness that God planned for you. And trust me; I had more than my share of negatives every day.

- Second – Stand on the shoulders of others. Look at what successful people are doing and copy it. Always be on the lookout for a better idea. We have two ears and one mouth—use them in the same proportion.

- Third – Don't be afraid to change. You have to actually implement the best ideas or it will be impossible to unleash their power in your life.

At high school graduation, Bud asked me if I would go to pharmacy school and take over the store. But I needed to shake off the dust of my past and move forward. I barely got into the University of Dayton, and then applied everything I learned from Bud.

I came home my freshmen year with straight A's – my parents almost fell out of their seats! Over the next four years, I got only four B's. Some people thought I was smart, but I knew better. I just believed in myself, watched what successful students did, and copied the best techniques in my everyday life. Thanks Bud.

Armed with my three-legged stool of success, I joined the firm that ultimately became Accenture, the world's largest consulting firm. For sixteen years, I went from business to business ferreting out new ways of doing business and helping other companies implement these ideas.

Early in my career, I was asked to lead one of the first social networking projects (before anyone called it social networking). We put in place a system to connect thousands of experts from around the world. The system costs millions of dollars and took a huge amount of effort to build.

When we turned the system on, it failed. The technology worked great, but the experts did not do what they were supposed to do. We regrouped and did more research. I found that we missed several key psychological principles that are needed to make social networking really work.

We added these key psychological principles to the project and turned it on again. This time it worked like a charm—it was a true homerun. In fact, the company who we built this system for is still using it as a key competitive advantage today!

# PREFACE

While life at Accenture was fun, it was also demanding. Among my clients were Proctor & Gamble, Ocean Spray, Hallmark, and Corning. I worked in Spain, Italy, UK, New York, Florida, Pittsburgh, Kansas City, and more. I left home on Sunday and often did not return until the next weekend. Typically, I was home only two weekends each month. Even though I rose to the rank of partner, I needed to make a change for my family. So, in 2004 I hung up the road and started several of my own businesses.

In 2006, I met a very nice businessman at a networking event who asked me for some help. His real estate business was going downhill and he did not understand what was wrong with his marketing. I called my good friend and business partner Bill Brown, and together we decided to go out and uncover the latest marketing ideas, techniques, and tools.

The world was changing with the growth of Internet marketing and social networking. We researched countless businesses and technologies from many different industries. We found that although many marketing techniques were successful just five years ago, they were no longer effective today. At the same time, a few leading-edge businesses were harnessing new marketing techniques through social networking.

From our research, we found several social networking secrets that successful companies understood. We shared our results with my friend, and over the next two years, he quadrupled the gross income of his real estate business.

Out of our efforts, we formed LGM3 (by the way, LGM3 stands for Lets Go Make More Money). LGM3 is dedicated to helping other small-business owners and professionals harness the power of Internet marketing and social networking to make more money. We have built our company on the principles that I learned from Bud:

1. Believe in yourself

2. Learn what is really working in the world

3. Implement what is working in your business

So dig in and enjoy the book.

Greg Pitstick

# Contents

# Introduction

Welcome to **The Smart Entrepreneur's Guide to Social Networking**. Here, you will find a professional's key to unlocking a winning social networking strategy.

We wrote this book for you, the smart entrepreneur who runs a small business or professional practice. But, before you invest your time in reading this book, let's be sure this is the right book for you.

**Read every page of this book if you are:**

- The small-business owner or business professional who wants to cost-effectively grow their business

- Someone who has the desire to harness the power of social networking, but is not sure where to start

- Someone who is not very technical and can't build Web sites; if you can send an e-mail, then this is the book for you

- Someone who wants a simple path to social networking success that is straightforward and easy to start

## Stop reading this book right now if you are:

- A technical expert who understands HTML, PHP, SQL, etc.

- An expert in Internet marketing

- An expert in social networking

- A business owner who does not need to see results quickly

- A large company with loads of staff, and a large budget to throw at social networking opportunities

********

Good, you are still reading! Then this is the book for you. This book was written so you can read it over a weekend and start using social networking techniques on Monday morning.

This book should serve as your overall roadmap for implementing social networking in your business. Once you decide to begin your journey into social networking, you will need more resources, tips, and training that we could not squeeze into this book. Go to www.SmartGuideToMarketing.com/kit and signup

# INTRODUCTION

for our free Social Networking Resource Kit for additional training, tips, and guides.

To help you focus on what's important, we broke this book down into three parts:

1. **Social Networking 101** – Learn what social networking is, why it is important, and how it is different from traditional marketing.

2. **Principles of social networking** – Social networking is not about advertising. It is about relationship building. In part two, we will share with you the fundamental principles and techniques that you need to follow if you want to be successful with social networking. Ignore these principles and you will be like millions of other business owners who are actually driving customers away from their business with social networking.

3. **Smart steps to success** – If you don't take action and harness the power of social networking, you will never reap the bountiful rewards. We have developed a simple step-by-step process that will enable you to be successful with social networking. These steps to success are designed to quickly get you up-and-running with social networking, while adding more tools and techniques over time.

# PART 1

## Social Networking 101

*Learn what social networking is, why it is important, and how it is different from traditional marketing.*

# 1

## What's All the Fuss?

If you don't know how to set up a blog, send a tweet, or join a Facebook group, you're not alone. Fortunately, this book doesn't require you to know any of the technical details of the social networking tools.

Actually, anyone can learn the technical aspects of these tools, but it takes a smart entrepreneur to learn how to really apply them to their business in order to make money and grow.

Give some thought to the telephone. The telephone eventually revolutionized the way everybody conducted business. However, when we first got the telephone, you didn't make money simply from getting one—you had to figure out what to do with the telephone in a very real, nontechnical sense in order to make money with it.

Even a casual tour of the Internet will turn up a plethora of invitations to engage in the social networking process. The terminology might sound a little ridiculous, but rest assured—social networking serves a very real purpose, one that can help you and your business make more money
.

Eventually you'll choose tools to use—but it's not really about the tools. It's about the strategy. It's about the road map you draw for yourself that will lead you down the road to growing your business.

Imagine being able to connect and network with thousands of people without ever buying a plane ticket or attending a conference. Imagine a scenario where customers (who actually *want* to know more about your product or service) contact you rather than you initiating talks with standoff clients who view you as just another salesperson.

All of this and more is available through the social networking revolution. You and your business have an opportunity to join the *millions* of people who have hopped on board, and to profit from this fun enterprise.

# WHAT'S ALL THE FUSS?

## What is social networking?

In a nutshell, social networking is about connecting people with similar interests so they can share, discover, and communicate both offline and online.

Social networking provides an easy, interactive platform for people to achieve all of these ends in a quick, efficient fashion that appeals to the busy, time-conscious world of today.

Social networking is a different way of using the Internet. You might hear social networking referred to by the term *Web 2.0*. This is because the Web originally was used as one-way communication from the Web site owner to the Web surfer. One might have joined a forum or a newsgroup, but for the most part, people searched for the information they wanted and sifted through the Web pages that popped up. The average person did not own a Web site or publish any thoughts or comments on the Web.

Web 2.0 has turned the Internet into a two-way street. Now, anyone can publish information on the Internet.

Amazon.com was an early adopter of this phenomenon. They allow any user to write a review—good or bad—for a product. These reviews are now very important to people trying to make decisions about what to buy or do. In the old days, of course, we simply referred to this as *word-of-mouth advertising*. But now you can hear the words from someone thousands of miles away that you have never met.

In reality, social networking enables people to communicate and network—activities that people have been doing since the dawn of civilization. What's different is that you don't have to be in the same place or on the computer at the same time to interact. In fact, you don't even have to know each other.

All of this is good news for you. Social networking is powerful. It enables people to connect both to friends they already know and to new people who share similar interests. It is cost effective, allowing you to reach into this massive network of people. It is also easy and efficient. You can post an activity once and many people can see it and pass it on—making it easy to keep up with everyone in your network.

Imagine trying to keep up on a daily basis with everyone in your Rolodex right now, with only the old ways to help you. You'd probably spend the entire day doing nothing but making phone calls or composing e-mails, even if you limited yourself to five minutes per communication. (The reality is, you would just end up not doing it!

The beauty of social networking is that it allows a broad connection with everyone at once, with the option to create more focused connections if need be. There is always the option to get more specific if that's what is necessary.

# WHAT'S ALL THE FUSS?

Some of the most common social networking tools you may have heard of include:

- **Facebook** – A very popular site where people can stay in touch with friends, family, coworkers, and more

- **Twitter** – An Internet service where you can "tweet" what you are doing and know what others are doing

- **LinkedIn** – A popular site for business professionals to connect with one another

- **YouTube** – The world's largest video-sharing site

- **Blogs (WeB LOGS)** – Millions of people and businesses have started blogs to share everything from how to bake a cake to political commentary

- **Digg** – A site where millions of people share with like minds what they found interesting on the Web

- **Wikipedia** – The ultimate online encyclopedia that is created and edited by users from around the world

Though each of these has a different interface and purpose, they all have several important features that make them useful social networking applications: the ability to post content or to comment on content, and the ability to 'friend' or 'follow' others in order to add them to your network.

# 2

## Frankly,
## Why Should I Give a Damn?

The biggest and most common mistake that entre-preneurs make is saying something that sounds like this:

> *"This stuff is just for kids to talk about pim-ples. I don't have time, and this doesn't relate to my business."*

Nothing could be further from the truth. If *marketing* relates to your business (and it surely does) then social networking relates to your business, too.

Social networking is, without a doubt, the most powerful marketing tool available today. It is also, when handled correctly, one of the most effective.

For example, social networking was one of the key tools our current president used to get elected.

In truth, we haven't encountered a business yet that can't use the tools and principles of social networking to really improve their marketing.

You should pay attention, because a true revolution is going on. Let's consider some basic demographics using statistics from www.beingpeterkim.com.

- Social networking has now outstripped pornography as the number one activity on the Web.

- Facebook has 400 million users—if it were a country, it would actually be the world's third largest (after China and India).

- Or, how about this strange statistic? One out of eight couples who marry in the United States meet via social networking sites.

- Eighty percent of companies are now using LinkedIn to find employees, which means the social networking profile may soon outstrip the resume as the primary means by which people go about displaying their professional qualifications.

What if your market consists primarily of baby boomers? Do you still need to get involved with social networking? Only if you want to reach the fastest growing demographic on Facebook—females aged

55 to 65. Of course, baby boomer men are also heavily into social networking.

Here's another fun fact: *Name every search engine you can think of, and then guess which on is number two.* Did you answer Yahoo? Bing?

You'd be incorrect—the second largest search engine on the Web is actually YouTube, a social networking application revolving around the sharing of video.

In fact, one study said that 25 percent of Americans actually watched a short video on their cell phone recently. Social networking has another advantage in that it goes beyond the personal PC or laptop computer. Social networking goes straight to cell phones around the world.

As I write this book, I am watching the Iranian Government try to regain control from protesters who are using their cell phones to share pictures, video, and stories from inside protests. You can't control this new genie; it is truly out of the bottle.

And just how much does this consumer rating, commenting, and discussion matter? Quite a lot, as 78 percent of consumers trust peer recommendations more than they trust ads. Only 14 percent of consumers trust advertisements over reviews. And who really listens to advertisements anyway? Ninety percent of people with TiVo and DVR capabilities routinely skip ads whenever they can.

Now is the time to give a damn.

# 3

## Help, My Marketing Sucks!

Many entrepreneurs are finding that their traditional marketing methods are no longer serving them well. Businesses locked into traditional marketing techniques still focus on trying to get people to 'know' their business by focusing on image or brand advertising. Many businesses are wasting thousands of dollars each year with yellow page, television, newspaper, and radio ads, direct mailings, and more.

Business owners who use traditional advertising hope that their frequent ads will make the customer think of them first when they are ready to buy. And for good reason, this type of advertising has worked for years.

However, traditional advertising is now *failing*, just as newspapers are failing, because everything has changed. Let's look at why traditional marketing is no longer effective.

## Your ads are being blocked

Seth Godin, author and marketing guru, coined the phrase "interruption marketing" to describe most traditional marketing—because the ads interrupt what you are reading, watching, or listening to. They are an annoyance.

The more annoying the ads get, the more demand there is for ways to block the interruptions. Enter the interruption-ad blockers.

- **Television ads** – TiVo and DVR have given consumers the ability to easily block television ads.

- **E-mail advertising** – E-mails must comply with federal e-mail laws (and good luck getting past those spam filters).

- **Faxing** – For a little while, faxed advertising was all the rage. Of course, now there is the *Do Not Fax* list.

- **Telemarketing** – Phone calls and telemarketers were never very welcome to begin with, but now there is the *Do Not Call* list.

- **Direct mailing** – This is effective but expensive. A good postcard campaign may only get a 1 percent response rate. The remaining 99 percent are thrown away!

- **Radio advertising** – People are now using iPods, XM satellite radio, or Pandora to get their music. If they *are* listening to the radio, it's probably while in a car, so they are un-likely to stop and jot down your phone number.

If in the old days only about half of the advertising worked, now the traditional marketer may see results less than 5 percent of the time.

## *Costs of Traditional Advertising*

- *Billboards: $700–$2500 per month*

- *Newspaper ads: $1000+ per full-page ad*

- *30-second TV commercial: $1000–$13,5000 for production and $5 per 1000 viewers for the time*

- *Radio commercial: $850–$900 for production and $6,000 per month*

## Now it's harder than ever to get mind-share

Mind-share (not market share) is the quality of having your business name at the top of your consumers' heads when they're ready to buy. McDonalds has mind-share for burgers. Dominos has mind-share for Pizza. Goodyear has mind-share for tires.

Here is the problem: We are bombarded with roughly 3,000 advertising messages per day. Our simple minds cannot process or retain all these messages. So, our subconscious mind protects us by blocking these messages from our conscious mind.

Think about it: *Can you name three real estate agents or three insurance agents off the top of your head?*

If you are friends with three real estate agents or three insurance agents, then the task is easier. But if you aren't, you probably won't be able to come up with three names even though there are probably 700 billboards and grocery cart ads that show you all sorts of names.

Why? Because you don't care about real estate agents! They are not relevant to you. Your mind can safely discard that information without even consulting you. Your mind already knows what is and is not relevant to you.

## *The Power of the Subconscious Mind*

*Have you ever realized that when you buy a new car, you suddenly notice the exact same make and model around every corner? It seems like everyone bought the same car you did!*

*Or have you or your partner ever been pregnant? You notice pregnant people everywhere you go. You can spot a pregnant woman from across a crowded store!*

*This is your subconscious mind at work. It is taking in all the messages of the world and discarding those that don't apply to your problems, needs, or desires.*

*With social networking and attraction marketing, you can put great information out on the Internet, and people who need this information will seek it out and find it—the subconscious mind at work.*

*But chances are, their subconscious mind is not on the lookout for you, your name, or your business name. This is why you will focus your efforts on your target client and what they really want (not what you want). Learn more about how to do this in Part 3 of this book.*

So what are your options here?

One, you can keep doing what you're doing; spending more and more money and watching it grow less and less effective. You can declare to yourself that there is "no other way," and keep riding that treadmill. You can refuse to learn other options and continue using interruption marketing, which...sucks.

Meanwhile, you can watch your competitors use the new social networking tools and grow. As your business decreases you'll have the choice of playing catch-up or going out of business altogether. Your competitors will continue to take just as much market share away from you as they can by taking advantage of your old-fashioned ways.

You wouldn't keep trying to run your car on a broken alternator belt. You wouldn't keep trying to run your air conditioner on a clogged and dirty filter. Why would you continue to run your marketing on a worn out, broken model?

# Secret 1

# The Rules Have Changed

*The rules of marketing have changed. It is no longer about branding, impressions, or getting your name out; it's all about building relationships and giving your customer what they really want. If you don't learn the new rules today, you will soon experience the effects of these new rules in your bottom line.*

# 4

## Isn't This Just the Same Old Thing with New Tools?

Sorry, social networking has totally changed the rules of marketing in ways that leave many business owners and professionals confused and scratching their head. Looking at it in its simplest form, the traditional marketing process looks something like this:

**Advertise** - You would do a bunch of advertising to get the attention of those who might be interested in your product in the hopes that they would buy your product or service the next time they needed it.

**Sell** – When the person called, you would sell your product or service. The customer may even refer to you as a salesperson.

**Deliver** – Once you sell your product or service, you still need to deliver superior results.

**Build relationship** – After a customer buys, smart businesses try to continue to build the relationship with the customer in the hopes of getting a future sale, either directly from them, or from someone they refer to you.

*******

With social networking, the new marketing process looks something like this:

**Attract attention** - You offer 'honey' or information your target customer would want or desire. This attracts their attention and gets them to come to your Web site, Facebook page, YouTube video, or to contact you directly. Your goal in this step is not to sell, but to get attention.

**Build relationship** – Once you have their attention, you want to build a relationship with the prospect over time so they know you, like you, and trust you *before* you try to make the sale.

# ISN'T THIS JUST THE SAME OLD THING?

**Ask for business** – You still have to ask for your customer's business. But you use soft offers that are built into your relationship-building activities to ensure that when someone is ready to buy, they call you.

**Deliver** – As with traditional marketing, you still have to deliver fantastic results to your client.

Once you deliver your product or service, you should take them back to the *build relationship* step and continue the process all over again.

********

In the past, most advertising efforts revolved around the traditional marketing model—the interruption model. *old* They "interrupted this program," on television, they burst in on the radio, and they called during the dinner hour. They drew customers' eyes upward toward the billboards as they zoomed by on the highway. Magazine articles were continued on page 139 to make room for full-color, glossy advertisements.

In contrast, social networking embraces the *attraction or permission model of* marketing, where you *new* serve the customer by offering information, teaching, or even referring someone to another Web site. Yet far too many Internet marketers still treat social networking as if it's the same old thing. They set their Twitter accounts to broadcast the same mindless advertisement 14 times a day and wonder why their marketing efforts are considered spam.

For many entrepreneurs it's hard to imagine how giving away free information is going to result in a direct sale. It's the exact opposite of what most sales reps have learned: *Good salespeople don't typically sell by beating around the bush.* However, most salespeople do, understand the concept of building relationships.

It helps if you think of your social networking efforts as being one big relationship-building enterprise, where your job is to serve and connect with your prospects and customers.

While we'll cover the psychological principles in-depth in Part 2, think about marketing from your customer's perspective for a moment: *When someone is searching on the Web, they are trying to find an answer to a question or problem they have.* Maybe they have chronic back pain, maybe they're worried about moving their kids into a better school district, or maybe they're just looking for a trustworthy plumber who can meet them at their home after work.

For you to have a chance to make a sale, you need to attract their attention and offer them an answer—a solution to their problem. You have to walk along with the conversation going on in their mind to get them to pay attention. If you try to sell, they will run away.

When you offer them information that they want, they make a connection with you. Now you have their attention. You're not going to ruin this fact by bombarding them with a steady stream of advertisements. No, you're simply going to continue being useful and valuable.

When your relationship moves from one of suspicious-looking salesperson to that of a trusted *yes!*. resource, amazing things start to happen. People lose the resistance they have toward buying. When the time comes for them to buy your product or service, who do you think they're going to turn to?

They're going to turn to you, because they know you. They may even feel a friendship toward you. You might think that this doesn't apply to a business-to-business environment, but ask yourself how many business deals have been done on golf courses or at networking events. *ha ha*

# Secret 2

# Most Business Owners Have No Clue

*This is good news. Most small-business owners and professionals have no clue about how to use social networking to build their business. So, now is a fantastic opportunity for you, the smart entrepreneur, to take the plunge and leave your competition in the dust.*

# 5

## So, How Do I Make Money With It?

Making money with social networking happens in a variety of ways. It can help you with lead generation, branding, PR, and customer service. All of these functions grow your business.

You can use social networking in both business-to-consumer and business-to-business environments. The tone and tactics you use might differ somewhat between the two audiences, but the functions are the same. If you're selling thermodynamic couplers to other businesses, you're going to take a different approach than if you're selling a 60-minute massage session. However, doing either requires a paradigm shift.

## Find your customers and let them find you

For most entrepreneurs, the world can be broken down into three groups of people:

*1)*
- People you know

*2)*
- People you don't know but who would want your product or your service

*3)*
- People you don't know who would never buy from you

As John Wanamaker said, "Half the money I spend on advertising is wasted; the trouble is I don't know which half."

A big reason why most traditional advertising doesn't work anymore is that it spends an awful lot of time and money bombarding the third group in the hopes of catching the second group. Meanwhile, all three groups try to block the messages in the first place. Social networking is fantastic because it:

- Helps people you know refer you to people you don't know

- Helps people you don't know who are interested in your business find you over the Internet

- Enables you to find people you don't know who may benefit from your product or service.

NB .✳ All from the comfort of your living room.

## The Power of Free Information

*Jennifer's Flower Shop sends bouquets all over the world for all manner of occasions. Lately, Jennifer has been trying to make some sales by steering people away from seasonal flowers, instead focusing on all the other reasons people might buy them.*

*To solve this problem, she puts together a Facebook page and a blog for her business. She writes articles about how flowers can improve relationships and solve problems. She also explains how specific flowers are used for different occasions.*

*She does not focus on selling flowers, but does have special offers on her Web site. One visitor finds her through Google and reads that the bee orchid was once a symbol of industry. He's been trying to figure out what to give his secretary for Secretary's Day and chooses a bouquet of bee orchids to thank her for all her hard work.*

*Jennifer may never realize that the order for bee orchids came in for that specific reason, but the fact is, the sale was made because the customer was able to connect a specific need to the free information that Jennifer offered through her social networking marketing efforts.*

## Cost-effectiveness

Marketing with social networking can cost less, even as it helps you make more money. Social networking is based on being found, and social networking services are generally free. The investment comes in terms of your time—time to post, update, and provide that valuable content. A television ad, in the meantime, costs thousands.

This is great news for the small-business owner, because now you are playing on a level marketing playing field. The ability of a larger company to foot a multimillion-dollar marketing budget no longer matters so much in an era when successful marketing comes down to how well you can build rapport and credibility through a free social networking service.

This means you can spend that money developing better products and services. You focus all your marketing efforts on getting your customer engaged in your business. You don't have to sacrifice the quality of your products. In fact, it's now vital that you don't! Your customers will be reviewing you and your performance online—and both sides know it.

Social networking opens new ways to build relationships with your customers, even if they aren't physically in front of you. Where the maxim of business once was "location, location, location," the new maxim is, "information, information, information." You can sell to someone in Peoria and to someone in Australia all in the same 24-hour time span if you simply provide the right content for the right reasons to the

right people. Thus, you can sell more than you otherwise could—beating your competition.

You can see the shift that is taking place from big-
dollar image advertising to customer-focused information marketing.

# PART 2

# Principles of
# Social Networking

*Social networking is not about advertising, it is about relationship building. In Part 2, we will share with you the fundamental principles and techniques that you need to follow to be successful with social networking. Ignore these principles and you will be like millions of other business owners who are actually hurting their businesses through social networking.*

# Secret 3

# People Don't Want to Be Sold to

*Social Networking is not about sales. If your focus is selling, then people will run from you as if you have the plague. Sales will come, but only if you focus on giving your customer what they want. This will require you to actually know who your customer is and what they really want (not what you want to sell them).*

# 6

## Stop Selling!

Jeffrey Gitomer, author of *Jeffery Gitomer's Sales Bible*, says:

"People hate being sold to, but they love to buy."

It's true. When it comes to the process of making a sale, people enjoy a whole list of things more than they enjoy being sold to. For example, people do enjoy being helped, and they do enjoy finding answers to their problems. They enjoy being taught and meeting with consultants who can educate them— specialists who can solve their problem or prescribe for them the best product or service at the best price.

Customers like to work with people who they know, like, and trust. Before you ever focus on trying to sell to a customer, you need to focus on getting that customer to know you, like you, and trust you. In these days, brand recognition is nothing without likeability. Today's marketing is all about forging relationships.

Let's take this example: You walk into a shoe store. You really need a new pair of shoes to wear to a wedding this weekend, but the salesperson comes up to you and says, "May I help you?"

If you're like most people, chances are you don't even think before you immediately say, "No thanks, just looking." Immediately, you feel even warier about making a purchase than you did before you walked into the shoe store. Your guard has just gone up; someone wants to sell you something.

So the goal is to become a consultant. The basic principles of becoming a good consultant are best described in Bob Burg's classic book *Endless Referrals*: "All things being equal, people will do business with, and refer business to, those people they know, like, and trust."

## Know

Of course, getting people to know you does go back (somewhat) to mind-share. People have to know you if they're going to work with you. Our minds are so full—so preoccupied—that it really is difficult to get the mind-share. The problem you as an entrepreneur are going to face is that most people just aren't going to remember you or your name.

38

It's not really who you know—it's who knows *you*. Later in this book, we will cover the psychological principles that will help you retain mind-share.

In addition, in the smart steps to success, you will learn how to present your business so *it stands out from the crowd*, avoiding the common *me-too* problem.

## Like

Why is Oprah one of the richest, most powerful, and most successful women in the world? It's because she shows us her personality. We have a good idea who she is. She openly shares her failures as well as her successes. She's not afraid to be transparent, and people love her for it. When Oprah says, "Read this book," people run out to read the book. Oprah is likeable.

So, show your personality. Show it on your Web site and in any videos that you have. Many people are afraid to do video because they're not polished television professionals. They're afraid to make a mistake. They're afraid that they won't look good. In truth, people want to deal with real people. Reality television has made it okay to goof up on television. If you do goof up on television, you are going to look a lot more real.

Another thing you'll have to do is share some of the credit with other people. People don't like egomaniacs—they don't like people who take all the credit for themselves. If someone else has a great idea, put in a link that gives them credit—send someone to *their* Web site, *their* blog, or *their* video. Take the time to say, "Look at what this person is doing, it's really interesting." This works especially well if you can collaborate with someone in a related industry.

If you're a realtor, for example, you might want to find some appraisers, inspectors, and mortgage lenders who are experts—professionals doing great things. You want to find people who "get it" and who use social networking. Then, you can lead other people in their direction. You have the ability to make yourself more likeable simply by referring these other people and by showing that you don't mind sharing the spotlight a little. You also create reciprocity with these professionals, who are likely to send referrals and leads back to you.

Also, this likeability factor is why we recommend that you hire a photographer to take a nice, casual photo of yourself. Take it in your kitchen, backyard or in a park. Take it somewhere that shows you as a real person doing real things.

Oftentimes professionals take pictures on plain, blue-screen backgrounds. You need to break out of the mold and take a picture of yourself doing something that real people do. This helps forge you into the minds of the people you are working with as more than just another overly polished face. People have learned that while pretty, things that are too polished are usually fraudulent. You don't want to choose an *embarrassing* photo or a photo of yourself drunk, but you can pick a nice photograph in a nice setting.

Another factor in being likeable is being positive! Nobody wants to work with a negative person.

Your ability to communicate and openness to other people is key to how likeable you actually are. In person, it's a smile. On the Internet, it is upbeat updates. It may even mean the use of emoticons (e.g., the ever-popular ☺). Just as your voice can have a tone over the phone, your social networking updates can have a tone that conveys itself to your readers and followers.

## Trust

People have to be able to trust you, to see you as someone who has their best interests at heart. They have to trust that you are not just trying to sell them whatever you are offering.

Almost everyone has received scam e-mails or scam letters of some sort. Almost everyone has bought a product or service that managed to fall well short of promised expectations. In short, the average person is more skeptical than ever.

You build trust over time by being consistent with your customers:

- Consistently publishing good information online that helps your customer, instead of posting cheesy sales messages

- Consistently delivering superior products and services

- Being consistent with your status updates, newsletters, and article posts

You can also build trust by being honest and true to your customer.

- Trustworthy businesses don't run "going out of business" specials every year

- Trustworthy businesses reflect the personality and intentions of the business owner

- Trustworthy businesses don't claim unreasonable results that no one could ever achieve

- Trustworthy businesses don't keep secrets and always have their customer's best interest at heart

- Trustworthy businesses have reasonable(or even unbelievable) guarantees and stand behind their product or service

How does someone new to your business find out you are trustworthy?

- Have good testimonials that talk about quality products and caring service

- Don't make your Web site look like a used-car sales commercial

- Use fonts and colors that are easy to read and use lots of white space on your Web site (Yup, this helps)

What's the quickest way to kill that trust? To put on the old "hard sell" right after you meet someone.

## Move your focus upstream

With the advent of social networking, building on the *know*, *like*, and *trust* principles is even more important today than it was before. For the most part, selling is still a numbers game. But the smart entrepreneur knows that they have to move their focus from the number of leads they get to the number of people who know, like, and trust them.

### *The goal is not additional sales leads!*

The goal is to meet more people so you can turn them into long-term *relationships*. Dan Kennedy, famous marketing guru, said it best:

> *"I see a sale as a way to get a customer, not a customer as a way to get a sale."*

Over the long run, building relationships is the cheapest way to grow your business.

# Secret 4

# People Are People and We Have Been that Way for 5000 Years

*Many of our social rules and behaviors have been formed over thousands of years. You can be very successful with social networking if you just tap into these fundamental rules of human behavior. The social networking rules are simple to understand and even easier to use, but they are different from traditional advertising techniques.*

# 7

## The Four Psychological Pillars of Social Networking

When you take advantage of social networking, you'll be tapping into the emotional basis of why people buy. We've already hit on some of those emotional buttons that you and your offer can push to get people to pick up the phone. Beyond those buttons, though, there are four principles or pillars holding up your marketing efforts. Ignore them at your peril, because if you do so, your marketing is likely to flop.

### Pillar #1: Give Before Receiving

We have a very strong social norm. When we feel someone has given us a gift without expecting anything in return, we feel powerfully and emotionally in debt to that person. This emotional debt is called *re-*

*ciprocity*, and we all have this very strong social urge inside.

Here's a case study for you from a good friend of mine, Bryan Casteel, a real estate agent from Cincinnati. An out-of-town buyer, Jo Ann, was a very nice lady living in the Nashville area. She'd decided that she was going to move to Cincinnati in about six months so she could be near her grandchild. She found Bryan's Web site while searching for homes on the Internet. She contacted Bryan.

Bryan got to talking with Jo Ann and she said, "I need about a $150,000 house that I can put some work into."

Bryan said, "Okay, great. Let me ask you some questions about that," and they talked about the Cincinnati area—they spent a while talking about what you can get for $150,000 in various parts of the city.

Then, Bryan said, "You know, I think it might be really helpful to you if I was to send you a book about Cincinnati. Several people I've worked with have found this to be a great book. I can send it down to you."

Jo Ann said, "Well that would be wonderful, Bryan, thank you very much!"

Bryan sent Jo Ann the book and included a nice map of the Cincinnati area. Now here's what you need to understand: Bryan *already had a plan in*

46

*place* for this situation and for other situations he has encountered as a real estate agent. He hung up the phone, turned to his computer, and added them to his system under the *out-of-town buyer* program, noting that she was looking to buy a $150,000 home in about six months.

That system automatically told his administrative assistant to send Jo Ann the book and map. It also sent regular e-mails to Jo Ann. Meanwhile, Bryan forgot all about Jo Ann; he moved on to other business and didn't talk to her again for some time.

Then one day Bryan gets a call from a young lady. She said, "I believe you know my grandmother."

Bryan had to pause to look it up in the system. "Oh, yes, Jo Ann from Tennessee."

She said, "Well, Grandma's going to move up here, but things have changed. I'm going to live with her now, so Grandma needs a bigger house."

"Okay, that's great!" Bryan said.

"But you know what?" said the girl. "Here's the thing: I was actually working with another realtor to find this house, and I called my grandma and told her I was looking at some houses with a realtor. She said, 'Oh, you're out with Bryan?' and I said, 'who is Bryan? I just found some realtor.' And she said, 'Oh no. You need to work with Bryan. He's our family realtor.'"

Bryan called Jo Ann back, and Jo Ann said, "You were so nice to send that book. I told my granddaughter to tell that other realtor to go away. I told her to call Bryan right now! He was so nice, he sent me a book."

Take note of this! Bryan hadn't even remembered who this woman was, but the reciprocity in this case was *so strong* that it continued to work for him well past the original conversation.

Reciprocity really is an intense thing. People will go out of their way just to relieve this very powerful emotion—that sense of obligation.

You do not need to have Bryan's sophisticated follow-up system in order to use reciprocity in your business right away! All you have to do is to be out there offering free e-books, free videos, or free special reports. You're the expert, sharing your knowledge to help your target client make good decisions.

The people who benefit from this will feel that sense of reciprocity. They'll feel that sense of relationship. They'll want to return the favor—often by doing business with you or by referring you to someone else who needs your product or service.

If you want a great discussion of this pillar, you should read *Yes* by Noah J. Goldstein, Steve J. Martin, and Robert B. Cialdini. This book is full of some outstanding real-life examples.

## Pillar #2: Experts Get More Business!

It's important to realize that we all want to work with an expert on whom we can rely. Experts have the ability to show us the best way to move forward. For example, let's say that you want to hire a landscaper. Who are you more likely to hire? Someone who just sort of shows up, or someone who you can trust to design flower beds that will thrive without requiring a ton of maintenance?

Do you want to hire just any cancer doctor, or would you be more inclined to hire the one who has helped to cure over 5,000 patients and has a procedure named after her.

So, your goal in social networking is to show your expert status. You show you are an expert by:

- Providing good information that helps your customer on your Web site

- Having testimonials that show you are an expert

- Using a consultative sales approach

- Declaring yourself an authority or expert

- Publishing a book or being on TV or radio

Let's take the *providing good information* technique. When people go to the Internet, they often don't start the search process looking to buy right away. They're looking to solve a problem and to get educated—to learn before they buy. In the case of landscaping, you may go to Google and search for *best low-maintenance flowers in Cincinnati.*

And if you found a really good video in which a local 'expert' was describing what types of plants do well in Cincinnati with minimal maintenance, you would naturally think he is an expert.

On the other hand, if you find a landscaper's Web site that is a glorified version of the yellow pages, you would see him as a salesperson.

It's also important to have other people declare you as an expert. That's why you need testimonials. Testimonials are considered *social proof.* They reassure people that you're trustworthy and that others have had a good experience with you. Nobody wants to be first! If others have worked with you and have had success, it shows that the next person that comes along is likely to have success also. It's sort of like a social credit report.

You can also declare yourself an authority. That can be a little odd, especially if you were raised in a household where you were taught not to brag. You need to shift your thinking; it's a branding exercise. Let's say you sell services that deal with getting rid of mold in the home. There's nothing wrong with declaring yourself as The Mold Authority or The Mold Man—especially not if you back that up with a whole lot of great content about mold, the different types of mold, and things you can do about mold.

# THE FOUR PSYCHOLOGICAL PILLARS

Authority status isn't something that someone else walks up and magically confers upon you. You can be an authority just by knowing more than 90 percent of the people out there who might be searching for an answer to their question or problem. You don't have to have a PhD or outdo everyone else in the world who knows about mold, lawsuits, or landscaping. You just have to know more than the people that come searching for you.

It also helps to draw attention to the fact that you're an authority. For example, one great way to get leads is to get an article published in the local paper. That draws a lot of attention your way.

We perceive people who have been published in the paper as being knowledgeable—important. It gets your name out. It creates exposure. You have to give a little to get a little, but once you give you get more than you gave by leaps and bounds.

Do you think it's hard to get your work published in the paper? Sure, if you're looking to get paid for it. But if you're providing well-written content for free just to get exposure, the paper will take it. There are always times when the paper, on its own, does not have all the content it needs to fill up all the space.

Besides, what is a newspaper except the original content provision model? The newspaper doesn't make money on subscribers; it makes money on advertisers. What convinces advertisers to advertise? Readership! What makes readership? Having a good, thick paper that tells someone it's valuable when they hold it in their hands.

Finally, if you really want people to see you as an expert or authority, write a book on the subject matter and get your book self-published. It is easy to do and often costs less than a few thousand dollars.

## Pillar #3: Scarcity and Exclusivity

Every Christmas there is a toy that everyone has to have. One year is was Cabbage Patch dolls, another year it was the Nintendo Wii. In the news, you will read about otherwise normal parents pushing down other shoppers to get the prized toy—or worse yet—pulling out a gun or knife.

This is scarcity at work. Scarcity and exclusivity influence us all. If there is a lot of something, it is no big deal. But if there are a limited number of slots or a limited time left, we get up and run to the phone.

You can put the power of scarcity and exclusivity into your business. In fact, your customers actually want you to put scarcity and exclusivity into your business. They want to feel like they got something that others did not get. It will make them feel good.

- **VIP status** – Offer a VIP option where the customer gets extra attention or services. Put a limit on the number of VIP clients you can take. After all, there is a limit to your services.

- **Gold and platinum levels** – Bundle your product or service into levels. Many business owners find that up to 20 percent of their customers pick the highest level no matter what it is. Kings Island is an amusement park near where I live. They allow their gold members to enter the park one hour early on special days.

- **Limited-time offer** – All of your offers should expire or end. This way people are motivated to get up and act—to call you.

The power of scarcity and exclusivity cannot be underestimated. Even after you know this, you will still fall under its powerful influence. Use scarcity and exclusivity in your marketing efforts and you will experience dramatically improved results.

## Pillar #4: Social Validation

Social validation is necessary because people act like herd animals. We like to move in groups. We like to follow proven leaders, proven systems, or proven products. Nobody wants to be first, because the guy who goes out there first risks something. That person gets to be the winner if things go well, but if things don't go well, then he becomes the loser; perhaps he ends up looking like a fool. Someone always has to be first, but nobody wants to be first.

So, people look to others to determine if you're safe to hire. Animals do this all the time. One deer puts up her tail and they all run. Fortunately, you can actually create this social validation, even if you haven't been in business very long. You need to create the appearance of being very busy and in demand. You don't want to look too available. You're better off renting a bunch of cars and putting them in front of your business for a while than you are leaving a blank, empty parking lot.

Let's give you an example. Let's say you walk into an empty restaurant. The place is spotless. There's enough staff to see to every crumb and to wait on your every need. Maybe the food even smells good. But do we stay when the restaurant is that empty? No, often we leave. It just feels weird! If nobody else wants to eat there, why would you? Unless we've eaten there dozens of times before and know that we've just come in during a slow period, we wonder what might be wrong with the restaurant.

Online, of course, you can't show your full parking lot or your long line of customers that are spilling out of your door. You have your online presence, and that is where testimonials come in.

Testimonials not only provide you with a social credit report, but they also reassure people that you've been busy. It lets people know they aren't first. Good testimonials also help people overcome their hidden objections—the internal fears as to why they don't want to work with you.

Imagine if you had a testimonial for every objection, fear, or question someone would have about working with you. Wouldn't someone else's words be more powerful than your own?

You can say, "We know Cincinnati" till you're blue in the face, but until you've got Jo Ann on your Web site saying, "I loved working with Bryan because he really knows the area, he really knows what he's talking about, and he helped me take all of the factors of the area into account as I chose my home," you don't have this pillar up yet. You don't have it mastered.

When you talk, you sound like all the businesses out there who talk about themselves. You sound like a used-car salesperson repeating empty promises. When you let other people speak for you, you present an entirely different face to the world.

How do you get a testimonial for every objection? Simple enough—you ask! Ask a satisfied customer. Give a recommendation of your own on LinkedIn, or ask satisfied customers. "Do you mind saying a few words about how we handled your problem differently? Do you mind saying a few words about the amount of money we were able to help you save?" People usually are happy to help if they've been happy with your product or service!

Another thing you'll want to include is stories of you working with difficult or interesting clients or projects. The Bible is full of parables for a reason! Everybody loves to read a story, and we remember stories. They're so much more powerful than dry, boring presentations of features and benefits. You'll probably remember the story of Jo Ann from Tennessee long after you've forgotten the specifics of anything else in this book!

If you put together a rush job for a client that turned out to be exactly what they needed, tell the story! Tell about what you did to make that happen, and the challenges and frustrations you faced while doing so.

## *Creating Powerful Testimonials*

*Testimonials are vital, but it's important to do them right to get the maximum amount of power from them.*

**Ask for specific** *testimonials. Think about the reasons why people may not want to work with you. What are some of the reasons potential buyers turn your down? Find testimonials that are the opposite. If price is an issue, get a testimonial that says, "Initially we were concerned about the price, but it was worth every penny. We got way more value that we ever expected!"*

**Use full names and titles.** *If you can, don't use the standard first-name-and-city format; it looks suspicious. Customers are well aware that fake testimonials exist. Mr. John Q. Davidson, President, Ecstatic Corporation in Gainesville, FL, looks more credible than J. Gainesville does.*

**Don't rephrase.** *Leave your customer's original voice, even if you would have said it differently.*

**Use photos.** *Use the same kind of photographs for your customers as you'd use for yourself—photos of real people doing real things. Ask for these photos!*

**Place testimonials throughout your Web site.** *Don't hide them away under some subpage where a reader has to hunt for them.*

Finally, online social validation comes from other Web sites linking to yours. It's good to have a lot of people linking to you because it helps you get a higher page ranking in search engines such as Google.

As more sites link to yours, Google recognizes that your content must be good and ranks your page higher. In essence, your page rank is a measure of how many other people link to you. However, there's also social validation involved here. A link is an endorsement. If someone else recommends you or gives you positive mention, it's going to be worth a lot more than you commenting on yourself.

# PART 3

## Smart Steps to Success

*If you don't take action and harness the power of social networking, you will never reap the bountiful rewards. We have developed a simple step-by-step process that you can follow to be successful with social networking. The smart steps to success are designed so you can quickly get up-and-running with social networking, adding more tools and techniques over time.*

# 8

## A Simple Blueprint
## for Social Networking Success

The biggest mistake most entrepreneurs make when they start to use social networking is going in without a plan. That can lead to a flurry of random efforts that don't achieve any kind of real results. Without real results, you will soon be disenchanted and quit.

The worst thing you can do at this point is to just jump in and use traditional marketing sales techniques on Facebook, LinkedIn, Twitter, or your Web site.

We have put together a simple process for you to follow so you can leverage the principles of social networking and grow your business. The process includes seven steps to success.

**Step 1: Determine who your customer is and what they really want.**

Before you start talking, you want to know who you are talking to. And just as importantly, what do they want to hear? Often small-business owners will find this first step both the hardest and most rewarding step in the entire program. Don't worry about getting it 100 percent right; you just need a place to start. In addition to your target customer, during the first step you'll begin the process of defining what you need to say to attract your target customer to your business.

You may have done some of this in the past. But, it is still important to go through the process because now you are really focusing on what your target customer really wants, not on what you're selling. As such, we encourage you not to skip this process.

**Step 2: Establish your social networking toolbox.**

This is where you're going to jump in the shallow end and start learning about the tools and how to use them. We'll cover the important tools that you need to pay attention to and how you should use the tools to achieve your goals. You will, in turn, decide what tools will be used—and how to mix and match them so that they all work together to form a cohesive social networking strategy that works for you.

**Step 3: Create the honey that will attract new customers.**

Now it is time to create the honey that will attract your target customer. The honey will be tuned into your customer's wants, needs, and desires. Your honey will attract new customers by providing information, education, or services that are of value to them. The most important part of this step is focusing on what your target customer wants, not on what you want to sell or what you think your target customer needs.

## Step 4: Build relationships.

Learn how to nurture new prospects into customers, existing clients into referrals, and gain repeat business with relationship-development campaigns. If you attract customers and then ignore them, you will not grow your business. Likewise, keeping in touch with past clients is often the cheapest way to grow your business. We'll also tell you what tasks to automate and where to spend the bulk of your personal time.

## Step 5: Ask for their business.

After you have developed a relationship with a potential client, you still need to ask for their business. You don't know when someone is ready to buy, so you need to place soft offers that ask for your customer's business on your Web site and in your various customer communications.

## Step 6: Get results with short-burst action plans.

It's time for the rubber to hit the road! By planning short bursts of activity, you will be able to put in place a fantastic social networking system. *None of these efforts will pay off the day you do them.* Being consistent is very important. In fact, it would look unnatural or odd for you to post everything you had all in one single day. Your plan will allow you to create a productive schedule and a series of actions instead of locking you into a mode of just looking busy with your social media.

**Step 7: Take checkpoints, refocusing on results.**

It is very easy to get caught up in the technology and tools and lose focus on what really matters: results! You get results by focusing on what your customer wants, using the social networking tools that fit your business model, and by copying what is working for other people. So, we take regular checkpoints to be sure we are on track and to make any needed adjustments.

## *Tracking Social Media Success*

*So much business relies on metrics, that you may be wondering how to set them up.*

*First, you have to define your success parameters. Do you want to increase mind-share? Increase your traffic or subscribers? Make the phone ring? Do you want to learn about your customers and how they view you and your brand?*

*Second, you should figure out how to measure your success. Comments, conversions, and links back to your site from third-party sources, for example, can all be viewed as measures of success that you can track and test.*

# 9

## Step 1: Determine Who Your Customer Is and What They Really Want

Before you launch a big social networking program, you have to figure out who your target customer is and what they really want. There is an old saying: *You can be a millionaire if you just figure out what people want and give it to them.* Sounds easy, right?

To attract new customers, you need to tune into the radio station WIFM (What's In It For Me). WIFM plays songs about your customers':

- Thoughts
- Wants
- Fears
- Desires

To do this, you're going to have to define some things.

First, you need to be able to understand who your target customer is and what they really want—and you'll need to look beyond their vital demographic statistics to do so. Second, you will need to understand what you are really selling. Finally, you're going to have to define what makes *you* different from your competitors.

Knowing all these things will help you determine what you need to say, where you need to say it, and *when* you need to say it. This is why you need to complete step one.

## Who is your target customer and what do they really want?

You want to connect your social networking messages with the conversation going on in your target customer's mind. The only way you can do this is to really understand who your target client is in great depth, all the way to their feelings and desires, how they dress, and how they want others to see them.

At this point, it's best if you try to describe a single person that you can picture in your head. You can even name them. Some find it helpful to picture a particular character from a TV show or movie, or from someone they have known in the past that has the exact characteristics they're looking for.

By focusing your efforts on a specific target or niche, you will be able to attract your ideal client through social networking channels.

In turn, this will enable you to:

- Position yourself as the expert within the niche

- Increase the price of your product or service (the more targeted your service is, the more you can charge)

- Focus more on the needs and interests of your customers

- Maintain a concentrated marketing focus instead of diluting your efforts to meet every need of every client and satisfying no one

Initially, you may think that you risk losing business because you're defining your target too narrowly. But if you focus on catering to a specific type of customer, and if you place all your marketing efforts there, you will soon reap the rewards of the clients who flock to you because you have what they want. And, you'll be able to do so at a much lower cost than trying to cater to a broader customer base.

Defining your target customer isn't always easy. But take a stab at it anyway, and then build on your results.

## What are you really selling?

BMW does not sell cars. Cars are the product, but that's not what BMW is actually selling. BMW is selling a driving experience. They're selling the feeling of prestige. They're selling a sense of safety and reliability. They're selling luxury—the luxury that comes from owning a BMW.

What are you selling? Are you selling comfort? Are you selling a good family life? Are you selling excitement? Are you selling security? Are you selling great taste? Are you selling confidence?

## *How to Define Your Target Customer*

*You want to look at several different characteristics when defining your target client. Use this checklist to narrow your description:*

**Geographic** – *Where does this person live? Many business owners will focus on a section of town near their business location.*

**Demographic** – *What are the common traits of the customer? These include gender, age, income, race, education, marital status, number of children, etc.*

**Psychographic** – *How does your target client think, what do they believe in, what do they want out of life? This includes their values, attitudes, lifestyle, beliefs, and desires.*

# STEP 1: DETERMINE WHO YOUR CUSTOMER IS

As in most developed countries, we have all the possessions we need. Even the majority of poor people have shelter, food, and clothing. So, we have evolved past buying what we need. Now we buy what we desire. And the product or service you offer is just a means to an end. It is our perceived end state that we are really buying—not the product or service.

For example, who wants a BMW? Single mothers working as secretaries? No. High-flying executives are the most likely target for a BMW. They want the driving experience, the flash, and the bling that comes with a BMW. A typical BMW driver would not be caught dead in a Hyundai, even though it may have the same features as a BMW. The one thing you're going to need to define at this stage of your plan is the outcome your target clients get by using your product or service.

*Important note – After years of hard work I have found it much easier to build a business with clients who actually have enough money to buy your product or service. I would advise you to do the same!*

## What makes you different?
Imagine spending $50,000 on a new kitchen with a remodeling company called Just Average Remodeling. How confident would you feel about the results?

One big mistake that some entrepreneurs make is they get in this sort of *me-too* mode. If you are like everyone else, then you must now compete on price. However, this can backfire in a number of ways. First, when you drop your prices and you don't have any-

71

thing else to offer, people start wondering what's wrong with your product or service.

Not only that, but even if you win a price war, you lose. The winner of a price war is the poorest owner! Who wants to be poor?

You can set yourself apart on a number of other factors besides price, such as:

- Location
- Convenience
- Speed of service
- Care of service
- Taste
- Style
- Niche appeal (for example, one fashion company specializes in providing modest fashions that still look great for Christian tee-nage girls)
- Reputation
- A different or new approach
- And the most powerful factor: the end emotion or outcome that your customer gets!

You first set yourself apart with a really good and short introduction or *unique selling proposition* (USP). A USP is your short statement about what you do that gets people to say, "Wow, how do you do that?"

# STEP 1: DETERMINE WHO YOUR CUSTOMER IS

Building a good USP takes some effort, but it is absolutely worth it because of the added advantage you'll have in the market. You are going to use your USP on Facebook, LinkedIn, in your blog, and throughout your marketing.

It is going to be the *wow factor*, helping you to cut through the clutter and get noticed in the vast sea of Internet content.

A good USP is:

- Short, about 10 or fewer words
- Not confusing—it stands alone
- Does not require someone to be an expert in your field to understand it
- Makes your target client say, "Wow, how do you do that?"

Here are a few of the all-time best USPs that should get your juices flowing.

## Example #1 – Package shipping industry
- Problem - I have to get this package delivered or I will get fired!

- USP - "When it absolutely, positively has to be there overnight." (Federal Express)

### Example #2 – Food industry

- Problem - The college kids want pizza fast (munchies)!

- USP - "Pizza delivered in 30 minutes or it's free." (Dominos Pizza)

### Example #3 – Real estate industry

- Problem – I don't know if my house will sell and I have to move.

- USP – "Your home sold, guaranteed, or I will buy it for cash."

### Example #4 – Cold-medicine industry

- Problem - You are sick, feel terrible, and can't sleep.

- USP - "The nighttime, sniffling, sneezing, coughing, aching, stuffy head, fever so you can rest medicine." (Vicks NyQuil)

### Example #5 – Our USP

- Problem – Entrepreneurs don't have customers seeking them out.

- USP – "Turning professionals into sought-after experts."

# STEP 1: DETERMINE WHO YOUR CUSTOMER IS

## Your short story

Once you have developed your USP, you need to create a short story or elevator speech to follow it up. Imagine getting in an elevator and someone asks what you do, and you respond with your USP. They reply, "How do you do that?" Now what do you say?

Think of a short story you can quickly tell someone in about 30 to 60 seconds—the length of an elevator ride. This is a short story about you as well as how you help your clients. The story should be easy to remember and repeat. It can be a story of one of your clients who you helped or it can be a personal story of why you do what you do. You want your short story to be genuine and from the heart. Tell your story to some of your friends and get their input. They may bring up points about you that you may overlook.

Use your short story to complete your bio on Facebook, LinkedIn, and other social networking sites. After completing this step, you now know exactly who you want to talk to using social networking. In addition, you have come up with a description of your product or service that matches what your customer wants!

Now it's time to dive into some of the social networking tools.

# Secret 5

# Tools are Tools

*New social networking applications like Twitter, Facebook, and LinkedIn are just tools. It is not the tools that are important; it is how you use the tools and how you use them together. If you focus on what your customer wants first, then the tools will fall into place.*

# 10

## Step 2: Establish Your Social Networking Toolbox

There are hundereds of social netowrking tools out there with millions of users. Over the past few years, several sites have become more popular and form the basis of your social networking strategy. The five sites you need to have in your social networking toolbox include:

1. Your Web site
2. Facebook
3. YouTube
4. LinkedIn
5. Twitter

Your Web site site is at the core of your social networking strategy. You will meet people on Facebook, YouTube, LinkedIn, and Twitter, but you want to bring them back to your Web site where you can offer them more information, build a relationship, and ask them for their business. This how your social networking tools relate to your Web site:

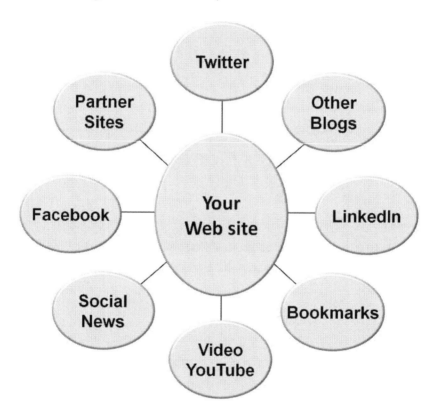

## Your Web site—built on a blogging platform

The term *blog* is short for WeB LOG. It is a site where you can post new articles, videos, or audio files to engage your customer. A Web site built on a blog is different from a typical static Web site because it allows you to add content and it enables your customer to add their own comments. In this book, we will use the terms *blog* and *Web site*. Both refer to your Web site built on a blogging platform such as WordPress.

Your blog is the most important site in your social networking strategy—you will have to pay close attention to the site. We call it your *content factory*, because this is where you put all the great information and offers you'll use in your social networking marketing campaigns. This is where you want every potential customer to come.

It's important that you do *not* think of this site as a personal blog where you talk about your personal life and problems. You really need to think about it as the new Web site for your company. Over time, you will have lots of great information for your target customer on your blog. Most importantly, you can easily integrate your blog into your other social networking sites, such as Facebook.

Your blog deserves a lot of effort, simply because it can be reused in so many parts of the marketing cycle. You can send people back to your blog through Twitter. You can link your YouTube channel to your blog and your blog posts can appear on your Facebook page or fan page.

All this, of course, assumes that you're putting in that expert content. If you try to do a corporate blog and make the mistake of using it as a sales platform, you'll fail here. It's okay to include information about the new product you're launching or who your new vice president is going to be—just be sure it is not the focus of your Web site! People want to know how to clean out their gutters in winter, how to navigate a divorce without losing their shirt, or any other relevant information about the problems you solve.

Blog sites are a great way to be discovered! When people search online, chances are they are going to use keywords related to their problem or desire. Since you are creating content about their problems and desires, they will find you! For example, if you're writing about getting rid of black mold, those exact words are going to occur in your blog quite a few times. When someone searches for *getting rid of black mold*, they're likely to get to you because you've done a whole article on that.

Here are a few sites built on blogging platforms that can give you an idea of what you can accomplish:

- www.SmartGuideToMarketing.com

- www.5StarHealing.com

- www.CamachoCigars.com

- www.BrookeGriffin.com

- SimmsFurnitureWarehouse.com

## *Tips for a Good Blog*

- ✓ Have article titles with great hooks that make people want to read on
- ✓ Have offers which encourage the reader to request information or contact you
- ✓ Use fun and lively pictures
- ✓ Create articles which establish you as an expert
- ✓ Stay updated! Blogs that are not regularly updated go stale and die
- ✓ Keep the feel of your Web site clean and easy to find; less is more
- ✓ Don't use a template or generic content
- ✓ Keep it professional, but include your personality
- ✓ Your URL (Web site name) should be about your niche—not about you!

## Facebook

Facebook has become the must-have social networking site. It allows you to do so much, such as connecting with associates, relatives, and lost friends. You will be able to provide short status updates about what's going on in your life. You will also be able to read a news feed about what's going on in your friends' lives. You can even comment on your friends' posts. Facebook draws users from all ages because it's so easy and useful.

We like to compare Facebook to a virtual block party. You can meet new people and talk to new friends. However, it's vital for you to remember that *Facebook is not for selling.* Your goal with Facebook is to build the *know, like,* and *trust* relationship. If you try to sell, you will lose friends. It's also important to realize that not every person or customer that you meet will be your Facebook friend—you need a strategy!

Here are some ideas for how you can use Facebook at a personal level while still building your business:

- Keep up with what's going on in the lives of your clients. Pay attention to births, deaths, weddings, moves, and illnesses. Comment on their posts, but don't neglect the real world—sending a real card every now and then has a real impact.

- Get new friends by joining groups and participating in discussions. When you answer other people's questions and do so in a way that is very engaging and useful, you create a group comprised of people that *want* to be your friend and *want* to learn more about you.

- Build a relationship with your clients and keep your name out in front of them in a way that is not pushy or sales oriented.

- Connect your Facebook page to your blog site. This will allow others to see your blog posts on Facebook the moment you update them.

- Make interesting posts. Everyone gets up, showers, and goes to work. Don't make simple comments on your day-to-day life— be interesting!

- Have a casual photo and upload photos that make you real.

- Use lists to separate your personal and pro- fessional lives.

- Don't get sucked into time-wasting applica- tions! You don't make any money playing Zoo World and Farmville. If you slip up and put your latest Farmville acquisition on your news feed, you can also turn off many of your followers.

- Show you are interested in other people by commenting on their status posts.

For more information on how to use Facebook to grow your business, simply go to www.SmartGuideToMarketing.com and download our free e-book, *Facebook for Professionals*.

If you have a business that you'd personally like to be separate from, then you can start a Facebook fan page. This allows people to become a fan of your business.

Fan pages do not limit the number of possible followers, whereas your personal account is limited to only 5,000 followers. For this reason, fan pages make a much better choice for a business account than do personal accounts. Use your fan page to give special offers and promote special events.

## LinkedIn—professional connections

LinkedIn is the top site for professional connections. LinkedIn isn't meant for your personal updates, it's meant for connecting with other professionals.

LinkedIn is a great site for tracking and building your professional contacts. It will also allow you to connect to people and, in turn, see who they are connected to. Go about this the right way and you can greatly expand your professional network through LinkedIn.

Your LinkedIn goal is to meet new people and then to entice them to your blog site, where you have more information and offers to engage them in a conversation. To do this, begin with a compelling profile.

# STEP 2: ESTABLISH YOUR SOCIAL NETWORKING

Your profile is paramount on LinkedIn. You have to have a bio that is interesting, makes you different, and comes across as professional. Here, you just might want that professional photograph of you wearing a tie on a plain blue background. Once you have the profile completely filled out, you'll want to connect with past and current associates.

In a way, recommendations make the world go around on LinkedIn. Fortunately, it's reasonably easy to get these recommendations by giving some out and by asking people in your network to recommend you. These serve as testimonials right on your social networking site. Again, you can connect to your blog and add links to your Web site, providing road maps back to your valuable content and offers. But you don't have to stop there—you can provide valuable content right on LinkedIn.

The first way to increase your content value on LinkedIn is to join groups. These will help you meet more people and expand connections by putting you in a situation where you will be involved in many relevant discussions. Answer people's questions and help them out. Once you've done so you can ask to be connected. Don't neglect the Q&A section either, where you can do much the same thing without having to join any additional groups.

## YouTube: sharing videos

Video is changing the way you can connect with your customers. With YouTube, you can post short videos for others to see. Each video needs to be 10 minutes or less. These videos are wonderful because they have the capacity to *go viral*. Not only can you imbed these videos in *your* Web site or blog, but people who like the videos can share them on *their* Web site or blog, which means more free exposure for you.

People love to watch videos, so this is a fantastic way to communicate to existing and new customers. How-to videos go over extremely well if you are in a profession that lends itself to that sort of video. However, even Mr. Mold Expert can do a video series on the various kinds of mold. He can show us what the molds look like and what conditions create the molds. He does not have to show how to get rid of the molds if he does not want to, as that is what he does for a living. He simply needs to make sure that his video points viewers back to his Web site so they can give him a call to come get rid of their mold.

Who watches these types of videos? If done right, the answer to that question is: *Anyone who wants to know*. If you're providing great information that solves problems, you'll find that the same rules apply to videos as apply to Web content. In addition, the fact that customers are getting to see you for who you are makes a difference. It helps foster know, like, and trust when you are a living, breathing person whose voice your customers can hear. It is different than being a photograph and words on a page.

YouTube allows you to create a channel and share that channel with other people. You need to think of it just like a television channel. You would not see a science fiction epic on Lifetime TV, nor would you see a NASCAR race on Bloomberg. To the same degree, you should not upload to your channel a bunch of funny videos that you found elsewhere. Keep your channel for things pertaining to your business. If you're a lawyer who helps people navigate lawsuits at the lowest possible cost, you can create the Lawsuit Survival channel—how to survive a lawsuit without losing your shirt.

Don't forget to let your social media tools work together. You can post YouTube videos on your Facebook or LinkedIn pages for easy viewing. For a great example, visit www.facebook.com/Pringles. This is the Pringles potato chip fan page on Facebook. A single viewing will help you see how Pringles enables their customers to share videos all about Pringles.

Here are some great video ideas you can use to build your business:

- How to – Describe how to do something. For example, an appliance shop owner showing how to fix a dishwasher.

- Product overview – Review a product. Describe its benefits and how you use it.

- Walkthrough – Walk through your business and describe your process. If you sell real estate, walk through a home.

- Customer testimonials – Short customer-testimonials are fantastic for any Web site.

- Education – Teach your target customer about your service. Make sure you do it from their point of view and include the benefits they get.

- Frequently asked questions – This is one of the easiest videos to do. Just read a common question that your customers have, and then give your answer. One or two good questions can make a fantastic video.

- Quick update or news – Give a quick update on something new in your industry or some new promotion you are offering.

- Entertainment – Be fun. You can put out an occasional funny video, such as on Halloween.

Go to YouTube and search for *will it blend*. You will see how an industrial blender company sells its product using YouTube (and yes, an iPhone does blend!)

If you can't think of a way to apply video to your business, you aren't thinking hard enough! On our Web site, you can see other examples of how people are using YouTube.

## *YouTube at Work*

*One of the most popular channels on YouTube is Blendtec's Will it Blend, a site that showcases Blendtec blenders.*

*The series of videos feature blenders blending iPhones, golf balls, rake handles, and just about anything else imaginable.*

*The videos are very entertaining and do a great job showing the capabilities of Blendtec's product. You wouldn't worry about one of these things crushing ice. If you watch just one video, you'll find yourself wanting to forward a link on to your friends because you just can't believe what you just saw.*

*Blendtec also has people submit ideas for other items they'd like to see destroyed in their blenders, making it a great way to engage their audience.*

*Search for "Will it Blend" in YouTube to see for yourself.*

You can also do a YouTube search for other people in your industry. Watch how they did it. Jot down ideas for what you could do. Don't worry if there's some duplication. Just because someone else has a video on how to clean a gutter doesn't mean that you can't add one. Nobody will have your same personality and presentation, and in the *know*, *like*, and *trust* equation, that personality and presentation is what is important.

# STEP 2: ESTABLISH YOUR SOCIAL NETWORKING

## Twitter: instant messaging meets blogging

Twitter is new and growing fast. Twitter can best be described as a combination of text messaging and blogging. In fact, Twitter's *140 characters rule* grew out of telephone text messaging. Other people can choose to follow you and your messages. All of your messages are saved and can be searched.

There are several ways you can use Twitter to grow your business. First, you can build a following by Tweeting information that other people are interested in. Tweet valuable links, quick tips, and interesting things that are going on in your life.

To be a successful Twitter user, you need a good balance—25 percent of your tweets should be about your own blog posts, and 75 percent should include good, general information or details about what is going on in your life. Are you beginning to see how the blog site remains central to the social networking equation? Twitter becomes a signpost, bringing your followers back to your good information. In turn, you will be building a list of potential customers.

## *Twitter at Work*

*The Treats Truck is a small business in New York City. They bake tasty treats and sell them out of a truck on the streets of New York. They use Twitter to notify customers where they will be, and at what time.*

*Here's a copy of one tweet:*

**We're at 45th St. and 6th Ave. from 11:30-3:30, then on 5th Ave. btw 21st and 22nd St. till 4:15-6 pm**

*What can you learn from the Treats Truck?*

*Can you create a club for your customers and send them good information or offers via Twitter?*

# STEP 2: ESTABLISH YOUR SOCIAL NETWORKING

Yet Twitter, like all social networking tools, is about more than talking. It's a potent tool for listening to and engaging with your customers. You need to know what your customers are talking about so you can engage them.

Go to www.search.twitter.com and click on the advanced button. Let's say you're an interior decorator. You could search for *decorating* and see what others are talking about. You would see some people talking about the decorating projects they are doing or hoping to do. You'd see others asking some questions about decorating ideas and you're sure to see a few decorators mindlessly spamming their endless messages that read like this: "I'm a decorator, call me."

You can even narrow it down to see what they are talking about in your own hometown or geographic area. This is a great way to get a feel for what's on your target customer's mind!

If you want to dig a little deeper, you can also send out promotions and ask for feedback on Twitter. You can use the search function to look for your business or industry. Reading mentions will give you a pulse on how people feel about you or your industry. It will also give you a feel for the problems people are having and the solutions people want.

It's a good idea to look at what other businesses are doing. For example, local restaurants can tweet out specials to help get customers. Maybe the restaurant is a little bit slow that night—suddenly they tweet a special, a bunch of their followers get it on their mobile phone, and they've managed to fill the house that night. Major corporations also tweet out specials. Dell does it; so does Jetblue.

Comcast has taken Twitter in a different direction. Instead of tweeting out specials, Comcast monitors Twitter for potential customer service problems. It then uses the service to answer those problems, sparing the customer the need to call the customer-service line. Not only does this free up the customer-service line—decreasing wait times—but it has done wonders for their public image, which had previously been that of a faceless, uncaring monolith who mostly jacked up prices and provided bad service (yet was often the only television alternative available).

## Social news and bookmarking sites
Social news and bookmarking sites allow users to share content that they find on different Web sites. Users can also comment on these links and share what they find interesting on the Web.

So, if you find something interesting, you can bookmark the Web page with a social bookmarking site instead of using the bookmarking service on your browser. You can use both, of course, but when you use the social bookmarking application, other people are able to see what you find interesting. You, in turn, can look at what other people find interesting.

Participating with these sites is a great way to get the word out about *your* site. If you're trying to connect to a lot of new people that you don't know, and if your target is already online, you should consider participating in the sites below:

- **Reddit** – Upload stories and articles on Reddit to drive traffic to your site or blog. The key is keeping your submissions regular to gain a loyal following and increase your Reddit presence.

- **Digg** – Digg is extremely user-friendly, which is one reason why it has such an enormous following. Digg visitors can submit and browse articles in categories such as business, technology, and entertainment.

- **Del.icio.us** – This site invites users to organize and publicize interesting items through tagging and networking. You can tag bookmarks similar to how tags are put on a blog post. So, if you bookmark a landscaping site, you can give it a landscaping tag. That gives both you and your users some context for later.

- **StumbleUpon** – Adding a StumbleUpon toolbar to your browser and surfing the Web can open up your Web presence to a completely new audience. This is a quick way to share your discoveries and meet people who share your interests, which translates to another way for you to build the *know*, *like*, and *trust* equation.

- **Technocrati** – You can increase blog readership by registering your blog with

Technocrati. Technocrati is actually a network of blogs and blog writers. Each day, the site lists top stories in categories like business, entertainment, and technology. Being featured can significantly increase readership. This site could prove to be the most important social bookmarking site for you, given the centralized focus of your blog in your social networking strategy.

# Secret 6

# No One is Listening to You

*Even if you get on Facebook, Lin-kedIn, Twitter, and start a blog, you will learn the hard truth: no one is listening to you. In order to attract listeners (and customers) you have to talk about things that will get the attention of your target customer and attract them to your Web site.*

# 11

## Step 3: Create the Honey that Will Attract New Customers

The sad truth is, unless you offer something your customer wants, you will not be able to get their attention. Attracting customers to your business is called *attraction marketing*. This type of marketing is different from traditional image or interruption marketing campaigns. They are set apart by their focus on offering exactly what your target client is interested in.

When most people go looking for an answer, they aren't looking for *you*. For that matter, they probably don't care about you at all! That's why talking about yourself isn't very effective. You're having a different conversation than the one the customer is having.

Your goal with attraction marketing is to get new potential customers to engage with your business—not to buy from you. After you get their attention, you can build a relationship and then offer something for sale. But up front, you just want to engage them in a conversation—that's it!

On the other hand, traditional advertising focuses on selling. When you try to sell, your customer hears "salesperson" and they run for the woods.

Obviously, you want to make a sale at some point. In fact, one of the major mistakes entrepreneurs make with their social networking is the fact that they never quite finish the process, never quite reach a sale—but the difference is that you're putting sales at the end of a process instead of right up front.

Successful attraction marketing campaigns all have some specific hallmarks that make them effective. First, attraction marketing campaigns are focused on providing information, education, or services of value to the customer. At every point in your attraction marketing campaign, your goal is to be tuned into the WIFM station—What's In It For Me!

Second, good attraction marketing campaigns work well on the different social networking sites such as Facebook, LinkedIn, YouTube, and your blog site. This is why the smart entrepreneur knows to start marketing efforts with the message instead of the tool. The social networking tools won't do any good until you have something useful to say.

# STEP 3: CREATE THE HONEY

## Attraction Marketing at Work

*Say your target customers are mothers who recently gave birth and want to lose the weight they gained during pregnancy. You've figured out the emotions associated with the problem. First, there's self-improvement; she wants to go back to her old body. Second, she has fear—she's afraid she'll never lose the baby weight.*

*You attract your target client by offering the free special report: Secrets to Losing the Baby Weight and Getting Back Your Figure.*

Successful campaigns also adjust to the economic cycle. In good times, people are looking for something that can make their life easier. Get-rich-quick ideas sell when times are good. Shortcuts sell when life is good. Convenience sells when life is good.

In bad times, though, people are looking for help, solutions, value, and protection. They're not feeling optimistic. They've battened down the hatches. They've tried the fast and easy way and now they're sitting in trouble. Understanding shifts like this is the best way to keep WIFM playing the right songs.

Most campaigns will drive potential customers to a Web page where they can request more information—this is called a *landing page* in marketing speak. On this page, you will capture your potential client's name and e-mail address in return for some free information. This way you can continue to build a relationship with them via e-mail.

Your landing page may be part of your blog, or it can be a standalone Web site. You put it on your blog if your information will help increase the number of people who sign up. Sometimes, response rates actually increase if your company name is not on the landing page, because people may feel they will get sold to if your name is on the page. Remember, everyone has a fear of being sold to, and people know by now that they have to be careful about whom they give their information to on the Internet.

## Examples of successful attraction marketing campaigns

**Offers** – Give away something to attract your target client.

- *Offer free information or services* – Create something free that your potential client would want. This can include a free consultation, report, kit, etc. Potential clients will contact you to get the free information or service. In turn, you get a potential customer. This is the best attraction marketing campaign, and almost all professionals should use it!

- *Education articles* – On your Web site, create an article to educate your target customer. Take your target customer's top concerns and use them to make an education piece that they would want. To take it further, you can submit a press release and send the article to newspapers, TV stations, and radio stations. You get free advertising and lots of leads.

- *Review a product or service* – Help your target customer make a decision by creating a review. A remodeler can compare hardwood floor to tile flooring. An exterminator can review the different techniques to prevent termites. A dentist can review various teeth-whitening techniques. The list is endless. The best part is that you come across as the expert!

- *How-to video or article* – Create a video on how to do something. For example, a remodeling company can make a video on how to check the quality of a cabinet or how to plan a remodeling project. A real estate agent can show how to prepare a home for sale. Post it on YouTube, put it on your Web site, link it to Facebook, and tweet it.

- *Offer a popular low-cost product or service* – Create a small product or service that your target customer would really want. The goal is not to make money; the goal is to get customers. It is great if the price just covers the advertising. The product or service has to be easy to deliver. Your goal is to get customers with whom you can build a relationship over time. A real estate agent can sell a kit to prepare a home for sale, an auto repair shop owner can sell oil change packages, and a remodeling company can sell a home inspection.

- *Offer a bonus or free gift* – This is a classic. Offer a bonus or gift with your service. For example, a dry cleaner can give a $10 gift certificate on the first visit. Think about how they sell cosmetics in the store: you always get a free gift with the purchase.

- *Offer a discount* – Try to avoid discounts; they are hard to get rid of. If you have to run a discount, use real numbers instead of small percentages. If your average sale is

$350, a $35 check is better than 10 percent off. A second-one-free offer is better than 50 percent off. Try to run bonus items before you ever run a discount.

- *Offer an amazing guarantee* – A guarantee can make a great campaign. Remember, *pizza in 30 min or less!* You can guarantee service, satisfaction, or emotion. Add your guarantee to your bio and tag line.

**Networking** – Work with others to attract your target customer.

- *Build a partner referral program* – Do people refer you? A builder can refer a real estate agent, a real estate agent can refer a home inspector, and an insurance agent can refer a real estate agent. Focus the campaign on making your partner success-ful! Give your referral partner everything they need to refer you: material, informa-tion, Web sites, etc. Good professionals focus on how they can help their business partner be more successful by referring cus-tomers back to them! For example, you can write up a very positive review about your business partner on your Web site. You can also have your partner do an endorsed mailing (e-mail, physical mail, etc.) where they introduce you to their customers.

- *Buy or borrow a competitor's clients* – We all know of a competitor who is going out of business, retiring, or just working less than be-fore. Find out if you can get their list of names and market to them. Do an *endorsed mailing* by having your competitor endorse you! You may have to give a cut to the competitor, but that's the price of getting the list and their endorsement. Help the competitor use social networking (Facebook, LinkedIn) to build relationships and promote you (be very careful here).

- *Network to meet new people* – Participate in groups on LinkedIn and Facebook. Participate in online forums where your target customers hang out. Answer their questions and provide links to good information on your Web site. Take the time to fill in a good profile on all the sites you participate in and have a link back to your Web site. Also, participate in live events in your community. Whatever you do, don't sell!

**Build a following** – Get out there and build a following of potential customers by speaking, writing, and inviting people to join your club.

- *Teaching and speaking* – Offer a class or speak in front of groups. It can be live or over the Web (Webinar) or phone (teleseminar). You are the expert and you will generate leads. Real estate agents can offer a first-time homebuyer class. Remodeling companies can offer a remodeling basics class. Healing touch practitioners can speak at a health club or at any event where their target clients are. Don't sell in the class, just educate. Team up with organizations that need content or speakers—churches, country clubs, gyms, local colleges, local governments, etc.

- *Write a book* – Books are the new calling cards. There is no better way for people to know you as an expert. Do you want to work with the average insurance agent or the author of *How Not to Get Ripped Off on Car Insurance – Getting the protection you need at the price you deserve?* Send a press release out about your book. Feature your book on your Web site. Use the book as a way to get in the paper, on TV, and more!

- *Be a TV or radio host or guest* – Many average professionals have become hosts on TV or radio. You can also become a guest speaker on the TV or radio. This works well when combined with press releases, a book, or a big event. Some people even buy the airtime and have their own show. You can also have an Internet-based show for free!

- *Offer a club or rewards program* – Most businesses can start a club or offer a rewards program. Examples of this are homebuyer clubs, frequent-diner clubs, oil-change clubs, haircut clubs, and coffee clubs. Send your club members special offers and great information.

- *Build a following online* - Use Twitter and a fan page to build followers who are interested in a topic. Drive the customer to your

Web site to take the relationship out of Twitter or Facebook and into the real world. Offer specials or discounts to your followers!

Do you see how attraction marketing can drive your social networking efforts? Social networking becomes the vehicle while attraction marketing becomes the gas. All these methods combine to give you things to talk about through the social networking tools. Discussions and offers will open the doors to the *know*, *like*, and *trust* equation with new people, which in turn leads to new customers.

# 12

## Step 4: Build Relationships

While attraction marketing is all about getting the attention of new potential customers, relationship development is all about building your relationship with people who already know you.

It generally takes far less time, effort, and money to keep a customer than it does to get a new customer. The core of your business will always be built on people who purchase your product or services again and again. But all too often, many small-business owners focus solely on the new-customer portion of the equation. Only existing customers are going to go out there and become eventual advocates for you.

The first step in creating a good relationship-development process is to sit down and split the people you know into categories.

You're going to actually create five relationship-development campaigns, one for each level of person. You're going to want to put more of your personal time into the people at the top of your list. Down at the bottom of your list you're going to use automated campaigns that keep you in touch with the largest number of people—your potential customers and past clients. Automated campaigns usually happen through automated e-mail lists (we'll provide information on how to set up one of those later in the chapter).

## Level 1: The advocates

These are the people that really love your business. They will get out there and fight for you!

> "Don't buy a car from that guy, go see Joe!"
> "Don't you dare call any real estate agent but Bryan, Bryan's the only one who knows what he's talking about!"

These people truly believe in you and your business.

# STEP 4: BUILD RELATIONSHIPS

## Level 2: Referral partners

These are people with a complementary noncompeting business. You might have sent one another leads in the past or you might simply be in a position to have that opportunity in the future. Any business that touches your target client is a good candidate for a referral partner.

## Level 3: Repeat clients

They come back and purchase your services again and again, and probably form the bulk of your sales. They don't go crazy with sending you business as do the advocates, but they are solid and reliable. So long as you keep them happy, you know that they will stay loyal.

## Level 4: Past clients

They've done business with you in the past but haven't been around recently for whatever reason. These people might no longer have a need right now, or there may be some other reason why they have not come back to you.

## Level 5: Potential customers

You will attract many potential customers using social networking. You need to continue to 'touch' them with good information to build your know, like, and trust relationship. The problem you will have is there may be too many to personally keep track of, so you may need to touch them in mass.

## For all levels

Add new articles to your Web site on a regular basis. You will hear many people tell you to post articles every day. The reality is if you post two good articles each month, you will be more effective than if you put out 30 bad posts.

Your articles should be linked to Facebook and LinkedIn. At the end of the month, you can take your work and create a short newsletter.

Make your newsletter fun, interesting, and worth reading. A big mistake that many business owners make is they send out newsletters that are *all about their business*. Most people don't care! Think about it. If you're an exterminator, do you really believe that most people would want to read a monthly newsletter about bugs?

The best way to send out eNewsletters is to use a tool like MadMimi, Constant Contact, Benchmark E-mail, or Aweber. Even sites like Vistaprint are now offering inexpensive e-mail marketing options that are very easy to run. Plans can start at as little as $9.99 a month—a break from free social media, but still more than cost-effective.

These programs come with many features you'll need that will save you time and enable you to reach a large number of users. They include templates that make your e-mails look extremely professional and a sign-up box that you can cut and paste directly into your Web page.

*Tip – Sending out real newsletters with real stamps will get more attention and grow your business better than eNewsletters. If you can't afford it, then you should at least send out real newsletters to your most important contacts.*

## Tips for Autoresponders

- Look for tools that integrate directly with your Web site

- Have the tool manage your contacts, add new contacts, eliminate duplicates, and delete invalid e-mail addresses

- Use a tool that automatically handles subscribe and unsubscribe functions

- Use analytics to measure the effectiveness of your campaigns

- Take action to modify campaigns that aren't getting the desired results

- Stay compliant with the law on handling unsubscribe requests, list the legal address for you company, and provide a way to be contacted

Used properly, these autoresponder tools can be extremely effective and can save you time and money. Let's look at the exterminator again.

Let's say he really does make the mistake of sending out constant e-mail newsletters about bugs. It's all bugs, all the time! He can look at his autoresponder's statistics and realize that nobody opened them after the first one, 99 *Termite Facts You Never Wanted to Know*. He can use that information to adjust his campaign and provide offers that his customer base really wants to hear about.

What could he work on instead? In some cases, he can just adjust the slant. *10 Ways to Protect Your Home from Termites* will probably be more relevant to his customers. So would, *What to Do if You See Ants*. He doesn't have to keep talking about these things, either. He can feature a referral partner one month, or he can talk about upcoming community events since he is, no doubt, community based. When the exterminator keeps his focus firmly on what his customers want, good topics will open up to him.

## Membership sites and clubs—levels 1–4

Start a club or membership site. Offer premium content or information to your club members. If you have lots of repeat sales, start a rewards program. Mail checks that can be used only at your business! You can use simple software to get the membership site started.

# STEP 4: BUILD RELATIONSHIPS

## Campaigns for levels 1–3

Those customers who are at levels 1–3 require a different level of personalized attention. This is when you start to break away a little more from the computer screen. Here, you'll reach out to truly build a relationship beyond the somewhat superficial process of providing great information—important as that is. These people keep your business running, so it's important to avoid neglecting them. Here are some ideas:

- **Birthday and anniversary cards** – Send birthday and anniversary cards. Keep sending them! Sign the cards and put in a little personal note. These, of course, are for the people near the top of your list.

- **Odd holiday cards** – Don't send out Christmas cards. You'll just get lost in the shuffle, and there's nothing warming about receiving a stock Christmas card from a business. Try Arbor Day, Independence Day, or Thanksgiving. Things that happen outside expectations tend to make people take notice.

- **Events** – Hold client appreciation events. Hold training events for clients. Whether it's a seminar or party, your clients will appreciate the face-to-face contact that's just for them.

- **Personal notes** – Send a personal note—it will have more impact than an e-mail will.

- **Phone calls** – Call your best advocates and clients. Take them out to lunch or out for coffee. Connect and listen—don't sell.

- **Monitor social networking channels** – Use Facebook, LinkedIn, and Twitter to monitor what is going on in your client's life.

- **Gifts** – Send a gift to your best advocates and to people who recommend you. You have to be consistent, and you can't go down in value over time.

Work out a system where your level-1 people get more of this attention than your level-3 people, but spread a little of that attention to all three levels. It's a good idea to pre-plan all these gestures in advance. You need to budget them into your year. Your clients don't need to know that it was send-out-a-note-to-advocates day, but you need to know so that you will set aside the time to get it done.

If you keep up with these activities, you will seal the *know, like,* and *trust* equation to the point where it would take a drastic, negative experience for your customer to break the loyalty you are building.

Though they might not need what you are selling all the time, they will come back to you when they do need it because they know who you are and you know who they are. We buy from people we like. We always buy from friends and family over strangers. Each step in this process moves you more out of the stranger category and closer to the friend category.

# 13

## Step 5: Ask for
## Their Business

After you have developed a relationship, it is time to ask for your customer's business. The problem is that you don't know when someone is going to be ready to buy! So you want include soft offers with your relationship-development activities. Good, soft offers can dramatically increase the size of your business without turning you into the typical salesperson.

Include your soft offers on your blog site, newsletters, or even in your e-mail signature. Each offer should have high-perceived value, be easy to act on, and should include a clear reason to act now. Here are some examples of how you can softly ask for their business:

- **Promotions** – You can run promotions that include free gift certificates, two-for-one offers, new product introductions, and more.

# SMART ENTREPRENEURS' GUIDE

Tie promotions to some event, giving a reason for the promotion.

- **New service bundle** – Take services you offer and create a bundle. For example, you can offer a Valentine's Day Package, Independence Day Special Bundle, etc.

- **Free trial** – This is a classic way to get first-time business. Let someone have a free evaluation or free trial (e.g., test-driving a car). You can also offer a free evaluation or consultation.

- **Referral gift** – Create a promotion, trial, or gift that your customer can give to people in need of your services. People need to be told what to do, and they may not think of referring you from just a promotion. These offers need to be targeted to past customers. You can juice up this promotion by tying it to events when people will be thinking about others, such as on Valentine's Day or Thanksgiving.

- **Tests or quizzes** – Have people take a test to see if they would need your service. For example, a healing-touch practitioner can have the test, *7 Simple Questions to Tell if Your Energy Flow is Congested*—a fun and easy test that will lead the person to buy from you.

118

# Secret 7

# Rome Was Not Built in a Day

A good social networking campaign takes time to implement, and you have to keep up with it. Think of social networking as a long-term marathon rather than a short-term sprint. Most professionals fail with social networking because they burn out and consequently fail to keep up.

# 14

## Step 6: Get Results with Short-Burst Action Plans

Now it is time to put your plan into action. It's very important to block out chunks of time throughout the week to work on your marketing plan. The only thing that makes social networking marketing work is consistent action. Stop doing it for a while, and you'll drop out of your customer's mind. Once that happens, you'll have to repeat all your hard work just to get yourself back to square one.

On the flipside, you simply can't do it all in one day, either. If you try to do it all at once, you'll quickly become overwhelmed and you'll never implement your plan. Taking things step-by-step is the best way to ensure that your success.

We have found that there are three basic phases successful business owners go through when growing their social networking efforts:

1. **Getting the basics in place** – You need to get the basic tools and messages in place. This includes a blog site and attraction marketing messages.

2. **Start networking** – Once you have the basics down, you should start networking for more business while adding new content to your blog site. You can do this online and offline.

3. **Add new tools and offers** – After you are comfortable with networking, you should add additional tools such as YouTube and Twitter. You can also add additional marketing messages to attract more customers, build relationships, and ask for business.

It is impossible to plan a complete year with your social networking activities. Most successful business owners find that planning four weeks at a time tends to work well and is achievable. Once each quarter, you should take a checkpoint (we will cover that in the last chapter in the book).

For each planning period, look at what phase you are in and write down what you want to accomplish. Don't try to take on too much at one time or you will fall into the trap of planning a lot and accomplishing nothing.

## Getting the basics in place

First, take a crack at defining your target customer. Next, define what your target customer wants. Based on your target customer's needs, go ahead and define your USP and elevator speech.

You will want to set up an account with Facebook and build a complete profile. Put your USP into your profile, upload your picture, and fill in all your profile information. Once your profile is set up, you should begin to make friends on Facebook.

You will also want to set up your company blog Web site and populate it with your initial articles. For more information, go to www.SmartGuideToMarketing.com/kit and sign up for our free social networking training. Link your blog Web site to your Facebook account.

In this phase, you should also define your first attraction marketing campaign that you will use to attract customers. This can be a free special report, free training, or even a free consultation.

You will also need to set up your soft offers that ask for your customer's business. Just pick one of the offers in this book and tweak it for your business.

Be sure to take your online social networking activities offline and update your business cards and brochures. Now you are ready to begin networking for business.

## Start networking

In this phase you should begin to network for business while adding content to your blog site. Plan to add at least two good articles to your blog Web site each month. You should write your articles to your target customer and their problems or needs. Don't just write about yourself; write letters to your target customer that they would be interested in. The article title is very important, so be sure to pick a title that is clear and speaks directly to your audience.

At least three times each week, log on to Facebook and put out a good status update. While there, comment on the status updates from your friends.

Social networking is about networking for business. You can network directly for customers and for partners who will refer customers to you. Partners are people who have exposure to your target client but do not directly compete with you.

For example, if you are a remodeling company, you should network with material suppliers, architects, designers, specialty contractors (such as plumbers and electricians), real estate agents, and mortgage professionals. All of these people have contact with individuals who may want to remodel their home, but don't actually represent remodeling companies.

You should plan to network both in the real world and online. To network in the real world, think about where you can meet the people you want to network with and go there.

# STEP 6: GET RESULTS

To network online, find groups where your target customer participates. This may be a discussion group on Facebook, LinkedIn, or a specialty site.

To network online, you need to follow the ask-and-answer model. You ask good questions to learn about your target customer. You answer other people's questions to meet new people and to begin the networking process.

Write good articles that answer your target customer's questions on your blog site, and then post a link to that answer when people ask a similar question online.

To network in the real world, you should follow a similar model. Ask questions and learn about the other person first. When they ask you what you do, use your USP and elevator speech (keep it short). Always ask the other person who their ideal client is so you, in turn, can refer them. Just by asking this, you will stick out in the other person's mind. Remember, the best way to get a referral is to give a referral.

Note: If you are not comfortable with how to network in the real world, I recommend you read the book, *Endless Referrals*, by Bob Burg.

Once you meet someone offline or online, you need to work on building the relationship. Use the techniques from relationship development to build a good relationship with the other person over time.

## Add new tools and offers

You should add more marketing messages and social networking tools after you are comfortable with networking and adding content to your Web site. Try adding new tools for connecting with other people.

- **Twitter** – Listen to what your customer wants, and grow a following by tweeting good information.

- **YouTube** – Add videos to your YouTube channel and embed them into your blog site.

- **LinkedIn** – This is a great place to meet new business partners (who may refer people to you).

Along with adding new tools, consider adding more marketing messages.

- **Attraction marketing** – Select one attraction-marketing idea from the list and try it. For example, add a few how-to videos to YouTube and your Web site.

- **Relationship development** – Add one new relationship-development idea. Make sure you turn your new relationship-development techniques into a system before adding more techniques or you will drop the techniques you already have in place.

- **Offers asking for business** – Add seasonal or special offers that ask for business. For example, add a Groundhog Day special.

# 15

## Step 7: Take Checkpoints, Refocusing on Results

Every quarter, plan to sit back and take a check-point. You should look at your efforts so far and ask yourself:

- Do I have my customer's best interest in mind? Am I creating good articles and information that my target customer will want?

- Am I following through with attracting new customers, building relationships, and asking for business? Or, am I unbalanced and focusing too much on one of the steps?

- Am I active, setting aside a few hours every week to build my social networking infrastructure?

- What tools are working and which aren't? Where should I focus my efforts?

- What new tools are available? Should I set aside a day in the next quarter to learn how other business owners are using this new tool?

Use this checkpoint time to refocus your efforts and to renew your resolve to take action—get things done. If you remember the three keys to success, then you will be able to use social networking to attract more customers and to become a sought-after expert:

1. You can only achieve what you believe. If you listen to the negative voices in your life, then you will never achieve the greatness God planned for you. And trust me; I had more than my share of negatives every day.

2. Stand on the shoulders of others. Look at what successful people are doing and copy it. Be on the lookout for better ideas. We have two ears and one mouth, so use them in the same proportion.

3. Don't be afraid to change. You have to implement the best ideas or it will be impossible to unleash their power in your life.

Thanks, Bud.

# About the Author
## Greg Pitstick

After being a globetrotting idea entrepreneur for 16 years, Greg hung it up in 2004 to spend more time with his growing family—four kids and a fantastic wife. But he could not ignore the lure of developing and sharing new moneymaking ideas. The growth of the Internet and social networking called Greg back to help other professionals and small-business owners learn how to harness the new wave of technology.

Working with his partner at LGM3, Bill Brown, they created the *Smart Entrepreneur's Guide to Social Networking*. It is a complete strategy on how to get more customers without spending a ton of cash.

Greg's irreverent, somewhat crazy style brings excitement to LGM3. Never boring, Greg is committed to bringing the best training and goal-oriented development to other professionals. As a professional speaker, Greg not only provides excellent training, but he motivates others to get up and change their world.

Follow Greg at Twitter @gpitstick
and LinkedIn.com/in/GregPitstick

# About the Author
## Bill Brown

Bill spent years at one of the world's top consulting firms working with some of the most successful companies in the world. He has coached executives, designed innovative uses of technology, and changed entire industries. Bill figured he was done with that life when he retired in 2002. Returning to Georgia with his wife, two sons, and an adopted daughter from Ukraine, he resolved to start several successful small local businesses.

But all that changed when Greg asked Bill to join him in coaching other entrepreneurs to use social networking in their business, this was an opportunity that didn't just knock—it knocked the door down.

Bill brings to LGM3 his vast experience of driving change and creating value at companies in such diverse industries as retail sales, metals and mining, telecommunications, the automotive industry, distribution, and even hotels. Bill has done work for companies around the United States, in China, the Philippines, and India, giving him a truly global perspective.

Follow Bill at Twitter @MrBillBrown
and LinkedIn.com/in/MrBillBrown

# Special Offer

**Social networking is constantly changing**, and new tools are always appearing and begging for your attention. Yesterday's hot application becomes today's has-been (think MySpace).

More importantly, entrepreneurs are constantly trying **new approaches to marketing** for more customers—some work, many don't. But when they do, **the smart entrepreneur wants to know** about them.

How is an entrepreneur supposed to keep up *and* run a business?

## *Keep up with The Smart Entrepreneur's Resource Kit.*

*The Smart Entrepreneur's Resource Kit* will **keep you up-to-date** on the latest developments in social networking that the small-business owner or professional needs to know about. You'll even get weekly **success tips** designed to help you effectively use social networking in your business.

**Sign up for FREE at**
**www.SmartGuideToMarketing.com/Kit**

# Resources

For the latest information on social networking, we recommend these great resources.

Our Web site is full of great resources for the small business entrepreneur. Visit us at:

To have Greg speak at your next event, go to:

## www.GregPitstick.com

Become a Fan on Facebook and get special offers and a first look at our new resources. Join at:

## Facebook.com/SmartGuideToMarketing

Our *Smart Start* program helps small business owners, entrepreneurs, and other professionals get started with social networking to get more customers without spending a ton of cash. If you'd like to implement the principles in this book for your business, the *Smart Start* program offers a complete curriculum that will have you up and running in no time. For information on the program and on how we can customize it to your business, group, or association, contact us at:

## SmartGuideToMarketing.com/Contact
or e-mail us at:
## Info@SmartGuideToMarketing.com

P24 Thought - can I market that I am new rather than try to hide it? "I have the "time" to work for you".

Made in the USA
Charleston, SC
20 October 2010